Book of Comfort 1

How the Earth Began, The Origin of Miracles, and a New Connection with Holy Spirit

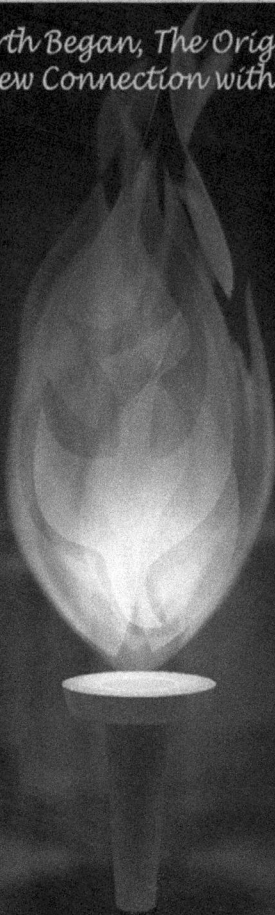

Rebecca Marina Messenger

Table of Contents

Dedication

Dedicated to All the Divine Ladies who constantly surround me...and to my Mortal precious Friend Cindy Cook.

Cindy,
You are such a treasure.
You have a heart of gold, a spirit so sweet, a mind swift to find solutions, the willingness to always be of help with your immeasurable talents.
...and you're doggone fun to hang out with!
The world is blessed by your presence.

Author's Note

In November of 2011, I was told about a series of books by Jean K. Foster and was guided to order them. Amazingly, the first one arrived the very next day. As I touched the outside of the package... little shockwaves of electricity flowed up my arm. The first book I received was *The Truth That Goes Unclaimed*, which is just one of several in *The God-Mind Connection* series.

The language was a bit old-fashioned, as the book was written over 25 years ago, but the words awakened a deeper level of understanding of Life, Holy Spirit, and how we can achieve greater spiritual mastery.

I began to use some of the suggested principles outlined in the books and it was only a matter of a week before things shifted in a huge way for me.

As my psychic vision became clearer, my spiritual life shifted easily into another dimension. I had already been a spiritual teacher for many years, but following this guidance accelerated everything at a very rapid, yet easy, pace.

I eagerly embraced the concept of having a morning meditation within my own inner temple and inviting my team of "Holy Spirit helpers" to join me. One morning in my meditation, there was just one being there instead of my entire team. I was surprised.

He wore a leather skirt with no shirt. He was very tan; very dark-skinned; black hair pulled back with a leather headband; snapping black eyes with a softness of brown. And although he never moved his lips, he asked to be my teacher. As always, I say, "Well I work for the Mother Energy (of course I believe in the duality) but I am here to express the tenderness of the Mother and that is much-needed. If you want to work with me, you must get permission from Divine Mother."

He told me his name was Ingrrid. I asked Divine Mother what She had to say. Mother says, "Learn from him, we chose him, he's very matched up with your energy, and yes, I know you have all these others. He's going to bring a new dimension of truth to you."

And so I said to Ingrrid, "Okay, I'll give you a try."

Ingrrid said, "Just give me five days. If at the end of five days, you don't discover the information that I'm giving to you is rare and enlarges your life, then I shall go." And so I did. This is how this book began.

At the end of five days, I did indeed find the information to be very valuable and I continued receiving information from Ingrrid until this first book was finished.

Book of Comfort took less than 30 days to write. It took much longer than that to get it ready for publishing, yet here it is, in your hands.

Love,

Rebecca Marina Messenger
October 9, 2012

Acknowledgements

Writing a book is easy... especially with the Holy Spirit team clearing the way. However, getting it out requires another kind of team effort.

I wish to thank my friend, Fritz, for holding a quiet space while I wrote.

I thank Andy Atkins for understanding what was needed for the cover art... on the very first try!

To my editor, Charlon Bobo... you are far more than an editor. Thank you for your encouragement and your fierce support of this important work.

Chapter 1 - Book of Comfort 1
Ancient Ancestors Took On Souls

Jesus was never surprised when he did a miracle. He knew it would happen.

It just was. Name your own miracle and don't be surprised when it happens.

~Sanat Kumara, Keeper of the Holy Flame

When the world was young, it had no need of human life. Earth as a living entity was very happy growing, blossoming, creating, becoming. The Earth communicated with itself and then... Earth became lonely, craving something else. This living entity Earth craved other beings, beings who would recognize Her as a living entity and who would communicate with Her.

The Earth longed to nurture and sustain life forms that had the capacity to appreciate, and so as extensions of life itself, men came to Earth, appeared upon the Earth, were created by the Earth in a rudimentary form. It was the Earth Herself who nurtured and divinely grew the man species until one day the Creatrix Sophia and her consort Father God looked upon this creation of the Earth, the living entity, and said, "Let us make man in our own image."

It was at that time that ancient ancestors took on souls. Before that, yes, they had life and rudimentary consciousness, but had not yet evolved to the place of holding Spirit as we think of it today.

Question from Rebecca:

"Are you saying that cavemen did not have souls as we know souls today?"

Ingrrid's response:

"Pre-cavemen, and even before that, the earliest man forms; this is what I'm speaking of, the ones that scientists can't quite identify.

Once the Spirit of Creation, source energy, noticed that Earth was lonely and wanted appreciation, steps were taken to alleviate that loneliness. First, life forms of animals came and yes, they respected the entity of Earth, yet they had no capacity to appreciate. Let us go back to the beginning and discuss this need for appreciation."

Ingrrid continues...

"Rebecca, I have heard you discuss this need for appreciation with your readers. Appreciation is not talked about so much and yet it is a very important emotion. Appreciation absolutely increases the value of anything both within and without; so in Heaven, so on Earth. One could even affect great healing by appreciating the whole body. The whole body would increase in value and diseased cells would be overtaken by the appreciated cells.

Yes, you may begin to incorporate this Heart Point Technique (see Appendix) appreciation into your healing method along with this Spirit-Merging exercise:

1. Imagine a circle of light.

2. Call a Spirit Being that you desire to communicate with into the circle of light.

3. Merge with the Spirit Being. Imagine that your energy is merging with theirs.

4. Send appreciation to that Spirit while being merged.

This sets up a craving for more within the Spirit Being and they will seek to be of service to you on the grandest scale imaginable. Yes, Rebecca, you did initiate something great when you sent appreciation to us, your Spirit helpers, in your meditation. Your appreciation alone caused us to barter for who would get to be your teacher. You have done much to help us on the Other Side with your Pink Net Technique (see Appendix). We love that."

Rebecca thinking...

Hmmm, why would great Beings of Light, great teachers such as yourself, crave a human emotion like appreciation?

Ingrrid, speaking for Azna, Sanat Kumara, Enoch, Data Dastagir Badsha, angels and my entire team of Spirit helpers, said:

"Appreciation is not just a human emotion and you say that as if being human is lower than being on this side. You know, you are just as divine as we are, so pay attention to your thoughts, Beloved. Your soulful self knows that you are divine within, but you haven't fully assimilated this into your heart; into your knowingness.

> *You know, you are just as divine as we are, so pay attention to your thoughts, Beloved.*

And yes, you are doing much good with your Flame-On Exercise (see Appendix), which we love, yet a part of you still feels that it's somehow lower to be human.

Just the act of recognizing the Divine Flame within you is huge and that is sufficient to attract the perfect Spirit teacher for you.

Yes, we as teachers vie for human students whom we can help grow, whom we can help be a light to others. We are not harsh with our students. As one who easily channels wisdom for the collective, Rebecca, as you learn to use what I teach you as spokesperson for the group, your mind will unlock many truths. Much will help you and much will help the world.

Now I will leave you for today. We have done much good, and Rebecca, I appreciate your willingness to give me these five days. I promise that I will keep up the velocity of good and useful information. I know that you don't tolerate unusable fluff."

Rebecca speaking...

Talking about the five days... normally when I go into my meditation, there is a whole group of my Spirit advisors; Mother Azna, Sanat Kumara, Data Dastagir Badsha, and angels of light. I usually receive information from them one-at-a-time. However, on this particular morning, when I arrived in my temple meditation, there was only Ingrrid.

At the time, I didn't know his name was Ingrrid. He pronounced it with a guttural emphasis, so it didn't sound like the feminine version of Ingrrid. He said that his pronunciation was the closest he could get to my English understanding of his name.

He was sitting there, naked from the waist up. He wore a leather skirt, had a muscular build, was of average height, dark-skinned, jet-black hair pulled back with a leather headband, dark eyes and his skin had a tinge of yellow.

He had rather round cheeks, just cheeks, not a fat face. When he smiled, his cheeks had little apples. I never saw his lips move, but when I think a question, he hears it and he answers before I finish thinking the question. He said he was here to be my teacher and I said, "Well I just don't take on any teacher. I must ask Mother Azna, Sanat Kumara, and my advisors if I should take you on as a teacher. After all, I'm accepting information from them and they are very high Beings of Light."

I consulted with Mother Azna and the rest of my team and I felt them 100% pushing me towards accepting this teacher. Ingrrid said to me, "Give me five days. If at the end of five days, you do not feel the information is worthy, then I will bow out; however, I promise to keep up the velocity of useful information."

Exactly five days to the day after receiving invaluable guidance every morning, he said,

"Rebecca, in case you don't notice, you are writing a book."

So, this is how the relationship between Ingrrid and me began. Ingrrid is himself a channel who takes the energy streams of all my team and easily funnels it into information that is readily accessible and understandable. He answers my questions immediately.

Chapter 2 - Trust the Divinity Within

Rebecca speaking...

"Dear Ingrrid, I want to respect your time. Do I need to always make an appointment with you? Are you available to help me anytime, night or day?"

Ingrrid replies...

"I do appreciate the respect of my time. You are my only student at present. I only take on one student at-a-time. I am happy to help you present information. I'm happy to help you with your clients. I'm happy to help you with anything that I can. Remember, Beloved, that I am yes, a master teacher and I am also a channel of wisdom from your own team of advisors. I step down the energy, making it easy for you to understand.

Our morning times will always be special times, set aside mostly for the teachings you are to share with the world. As you get more and more at ease with my presence, we shall do more together. I am here to be your teacher and I am here to help you become more of a master than you are now, for Rebecca, you are already a master at much.

You don't see it perhaps, and like you, I had never considered myself a master until the Holy Spirit Council elected me. I do not speak these words for flattery. I speak truth."

So I questioned:

"In what ways am I a master now?"

Ingrrid replies...

"You are a master in that you care deeply for those you feel are in your charge, your readers. You seek information that will help them.

Yes, you can get a bit aggravated with them sometimes when they remain babies and don't want to move. Any mother would, and yet you always uphold their best interest. There is no trickery in your heart. You follow your own heart and teach others to do the same. Another great way that you are a master is that you literally leap out in faith, never requiring any proof. This, you know. No one that we know of on the planet right now trusts as completely as you do. When you receive guidance, you never question it, even if it sounds kind of crazy.

Accepting information from a half-clothed man might seem crazy to some and yet you embrace it with your whole heart.

You trust the Divinity within you. You trust that Divinity recognizes the Light. So please, Rebecca, do not be harsh with yourself for your shortcomings or what you consider your faults. Do you think every mastery candidate is already there? Be gentle with yourself. My words are not designed to bring false compliments. I will certainly point out something you need to focus upon.

When I look at you beautiful Rebecca, I see energy patterns. I see where you are strong, strongest, and I see where you could use some uplifting and even some repairs."

Rebecca speaking...

By the way, I will teach you how, dear reader, to effect energy repairs when you are ready. In that moment, I asked Ingrrid that any miracles coming forth in my live meetings will not seem like magic, but a natural progression from Spirit. I will know that this is possible and it will simply be, just like it was with Jesus.

> *How funny it would have been if Jesus said, 'Oh my God, I can't believe I turned that water into wine'?*

Ingrrid answers...

"Yes, that is correct. Jesus was never surprised when he did a miracle. Some were planned; most were spontaneous. How funny it would have been if Jesus said, 'Oh my God, I can't believe I turned that water into wine'? There are masters on Earth today. There have always been. These masters learned how to do what seemed like miracles, yet it was matter-of-fact to them. Sai Baba plucks ash from the air and causes objects to appear. He is no magician. He is a master on Earth. All masters have their specialty, their unique message, and most have followers.

The gift of mastery can be gifted from a master to a student. However, this is rarely done, for it is only when the heart is right that this gift of mastery can be given. It is only when the eternal flame within is recognized and fully aligned that a master can bestow the gift of mastery upon a student. Mostly, mastery is learned from living. You, Rebecca, have two years in training with me and then another teacher will come."

Rebecca asked...

"May I begin to do miracles in my services very soon?"

Ingrrid replies...

"We know that you only want a miracle that benefits people. Not being slain in the Spirit, as an example, just for show unless that causes healing to occur. You do get to choose, so what kind of miracle do you want to happen? Choose wisely."

Rebccca speaking...

So, as a wise student, I asked my esteemed teacher, "Sir, what do you recommend? You know my heart and you know the hearts of the people who attend my meetings. What would do them the most good?"

Ingrrid replies...

"Thank you for asking me. The miracles can change. There can be several types of miracles in each service. When you teach them how to build an inner temple where they can create their own miracles, this itself is a miracle gift. Teaching seekers to look within their own heart; this is truly a miracle.

Physical healings will occur, yet they pale in comparison to the heart-healings that are occurring even as our side prepares the people who will attend your events. Did you think you were doing this all alone, Rebecca? Never."

24

Chapter 3 - The Tiniest Flicker of Trust Can Cause Miracles

This morning as I made coffee, I saw a hummingbird that was joined by another and then another, drinking at the fountain in my garden. I have seen one hummingbird before and I have seen two, but I have never seen three. So, I just took notice, made my coffee and went into my office to begin my morning dictation with Ingrrid.

Ingrrid begins...

"The source within calls to the sources without. There is great power here. This teaching will help many to understand that you cannot create anything from completely empty space. There must be an element of trust. Notice I said 'an element.' Just the tiniest flicker of trust has merit. A spark of trust can cause great miracles to occur. This is what Jesus meant when he said, 'If you have faith as a tiny mustard seed, you can say unto this mountain, be thou cast into the sea and it shall be so.' If beings hear these instructions and follow them, even

> The source within calls to the sources without.

though they have doubt, they will obtain great benefits; for new laws are being set in place, new laws for the golden age of spiritual progress. All the old tried-and-true laws will take on new meaning. They are no longer static, for they were formed for a different age."

Rebecca speaking...

"Can you give me an example of an old law and how it might be changed?"

Ingrrid answers...

"Giving and receiving. This law, of course, has been misunderstood for ages. It has been taught that this law meant to give and give and give and give and wait for the receiving. There has even been teaching that it is better to give than to receive. The new version of this law states that 'receiving is the key to giving.'

How does this work? First, be open to receive guidance from your own inner wisdom and from your spirit partners. Then and only then shall you be qualified to give. Now, I am speaking of spiritual gifts and knowledge, yet this can be applied to physical things as well. Ask for your financial needs to be met first, and then give unto others as you receive guidance from your inner wisdom or from spirit helpers."

Rebecca speaking...

"What about the teaching that 10% of our sustenance or income belongs to God?"

Ingrrid answers...

"In actuality, 100% of everything belongs to Source, for you are Source, so would you give 10% to something outside yourself? True giving, whether to God, to church or man comes from inside the heart.

Here we go back to the law. The key to giving is receiving. How does this work? You receive guidance before giving; guidance from within your heart. Never give to anyone or any group out of guilt. Check in with your heart and you will find ease-of-giving when you first receive your own guidance."

Rebecca speaking...

"But Ingrrid, it doesn't hurt to give out of guilt, does it?"

Ingrrid answers...

"Yes, it absolutely, most certainly does hurt to give out of guilt. Listen. Listen with your heart. There is already in place a perfect plan for the receiving and giving to be in beautiful balance, like two kids of equal weight on a see-saw. When you give out of guilt, you make one kid heavier than the other, so one kid is stuck up in the air and the other kid is stuck down on the ground.

When all is in balance by tuning into your guidance, perfect harmony ensues. Yes, people who are hungry are fed. Yes, people who need clothing are clothed. This applies both to spiritual principles and to physical principles.

A perfect prayer each day would be:

'Show me where I can receive today and then show me where I can give today.'

Now, some are afraid to ask, 'show me where I can give today,' for fear that perhaps they will be guided to give more than they're comfortable with. Beloved, this can never happen when you activate the law in the way it is being presented here. Just try it and you will find perfect balance.

What is important here is to keep your focus on your only true governor: your heart. Resist looking outside yourself by saying, 'Well, look at those big corporations. I think they should be giving more.' Look only to yourself, to your heart, for guidance in first receiving and then giving.

Know this, Beloved: the giving is not always in monetary terms. Give of your heart, but first receive more love into your heart. Receive more self-care and self-nurturing. Be open to receiving and the giving will spill forth from you so spontaneously, for it is much easier to give from a sense of gratitude than it is from a sense of guilt."

Rebecca speaking...

"A good Heart Point Technique exercise would be to hold the HPT position (see Appendix) and ask, 'What shall I receive today?' As you are asking, be sure to ignite the Light of God to the depths of your heart center. Note what comes up, then hold the HPT position again and ask, 'What shall I give today?' In both cases, some action may need to be taken."

Chapter 4 - Will This Shifting Be Enough To Forestall Earth Changes?

I began my meditation by forming a Circle of Light. Ingrrid joins me and he has a curious-looking fellow with him: primitive, hairy, big, and wearing animal skins. Ingrrid introduces him as Paul, the Ancient One (not to be confused with Paul the Apostle).

Now, as has become our custom, I merged with Ingrrid and anatomically aligned our receiving and giving information centers. He said, "No, don't merge with Paul the Ancient One," and I did not. In some exercises, when perhaps Jesus or Enoch or someone joined our circle, we three merged for ease of communication.

This time Ingrrid said, "Paul the Ancient One is here to show you something." So Ingrrid begins, "A new era is now dawning. One that brings both blessing and triumph, also changes, yes. Some Earth changes are necessary, and this will be a challenging time.

So challenging in fact, that many may elect to leave their physical bodies. The Mother energy has been very busy because the spirits have lost confidence that we will choose to shift.

Ingrrid continues...

"Many in the Spirit world, including nature Spirits and divas, had lost hope that enough of the consciousness of mankind would wake up to prevent the great calamities that have been prophesied. Doubts were heavy on our hearts.

The consciousness of man—collectively, the greater whole—would remain in darkness and not believe in Spirit. Science has been the fashion of the day. If it cannot be proven scientifically, then it has no merit. Now, thanks to the influx of the great Mother energy, things are shifting and this change is coming now at an accelerated rate.

To a great degree, this shifting is due to the new-thought movement. Minds and hearts are opening once again to the deeper, more satisfying, truths of Spirit."

Rebecca speaking...

"Can you give me an example of how you see us, as a whole, shifting for the better?"

Ingrrid replies...

"Yes, indeed. Even in the very young, we see teachings of respecting others. Teachings against taking from others by force, teachings of not calling others damaging names. We are pleased to see children striving not to hurt one another."

Rebecca speaking...

"Will this shifting be enough to forestall the Earth changes?"

Ingrrid replies...

"Earth changes are already happening; already in motion. Many have already occurred. In the very beginning, the Earth was created as a playground, a merciful place of rest and relaxation for Spirit beings and those from beyond your world. The Earth is a living entity and sought to make Herself more and more beautiful, thereby bringing more pleasure to herself and to those who visited. Earth saw that life was good and Earth sought to create an image of Herself.

Earth wanted offspring that could communicate in and of themselves. Earth created many life forms, seeking always that one that could communicate consciously with Her... seeking appreciation. It was then that Source in the duality said, 'Let us make men in our own image,' and the first souls began to inhabit the forms of men.

Paul the Ancient One—primitively dressed in skins—moved forward; not completely aware. This Ancient One—one of the first creations—was indeed part of the Earth. He could merge with trees to hide himself. Paul the Ancient One did not speak to me with his voice, but he spoke to me in pictures, showing that if he was in fear of attack, he could arrange his molecules to blend in with the rocks, blend in with the trees, and therefore escape annihilation.

This was considered an easy, normal, natural thing to do. He did not consider it any kind of miracle. It was the Earth caring for him. Paul the Ancient One knew nothing of Science. He only knew he was a child of the Earth, a part of it in every way. The Earth fed him, clothed him, and sheltered him from danger. He simply accepted the Earth as Mother."

Rebecca asked...

"When did things start to go sour for the Earth-man relationship?"

Ingrrid answers...

"When man discovered things had bartering value. It started off small with even exchanges like *you give me some of your fruit and I will give you equal amounts of my vegetables.* This was okay, but then a malevolent force crept in: *maybe I can trick my neighbor into giving me more of his harvest in exchange for less of mine so that I will have more.* This malevolence took root in human nature and crept forward in time. The greatest dropping off place or era began when man discovered gold and other precious metals.

It wasn't that the living entity of Earth minded sharing the beauty She had created, it was the way it began to be taken with no respect, with no appreciation of how it was created, and especially, absolutely, no energy of exchange.

34

The law of even exchange is one of the laws that will stand the test of time.

When one takes anything with no thought of appreciation to the giver or in the Earth's case, the Creator, a huge imbalance is created; a vacuum that may lie dormant for years; a vacuum that will try and hold itself as long as it can, but a vacuum none-the-less.

Even now, there are many, many vacuums; dangerous longings that are sitting, simmering, needing relief. This is one of the primary causes of shifting plates in the Earth.

Now, let us proceed in talking of the Earth's treasures and how they can be restored. Let us explore the releasing of the vacuums created within, with as little trauma as possible. The Earth is not angry. The Earth is hurt, for it has not been recognized and acknowledged as a living, creative, nurturing entity.

Earth has been robbed with no thought of energy exchange. She is indeed hurting; the entity called Earth does not desire to destroy, not at all. It does not desire to heave and sigh and spew mankind into the ethers. This entity called Earth desires companionship, harmony, and most of all, appreciation for Her creative endeavors."

Rebecca speaking...

"Ingrrid, don't you feel people are trying to return to the respect of our Earth Mother?"

Ingrrid replies...

"Yes, they are trying the ways of ancient native cultures. Many cultures even now still bring offerings to Earth Mother–tobacco, ash, flowers, praises, prayers. Realize this: **the actions of indigenous peoples through the ages have stayed the hand of much greater Earth shifting.**

These cultures understand the law of energy exchange. This movement back to the ancient ways is what will save this planet, our Earth Mother. If you take our advice and Her advice, you will find the birthing of the next golden age to be far less painful than if left to unfold with this newly-recognized, yet ancient, consciousness.

When you take something from the Earth, put something back. Better yet, offer something before taking anything. This could come under the heading of the new law on giving and receiving. Receive first in order to give in better balance. Receive guidance from Spirit before taking anything.

Receive guidance on what best to offer in exchange. Become aware that the Earth is a living entity that craves fellowship. Fellowship is never one-sided. Fellowship is interactive."

Rebecca asked...

"Ingrrid, we need a practical application of this. I don't like to hear words with no solutions. Tell us how we can effect more gratitude. How can we begin to have fellowship with the Earth?"

Ingrrid says...

"I will give you some examples. Some of these ways may apply to everyone; some may apply to only a few.

Number one: if your consciousness has ever sneered at the practices of native peoples, whose customs honored the Earth, apologize in Spirit. These truth-keepers have been keeping you safe.

Number two: think of things you and your ancestors may have rudely taken from the Earth with no exchange. Seek forgiveness and send blessings in exchange.

Number two: think of things you and your ancestors may have rudely taken from the Earth with no exchange. Seek forgiveness and send blessings in exchange.

Number three: begin to appreciate everything about the Earth. Appreciate the atmosphere; *I appreciate breathing.* Appreciate the soil; *I appreciate the life-giving elements there.* Appreciate the water; *I appreciate the water, the very essence of man.*

The creativeness of Earth; *I appreciate how the wild things grow with no attention from man, no interference and no so-called intervention.* Realize this: the Earth–this living creative entity–wants to be your partner, wants to be your Beloved. Earth wants to be recognized as an equal, creative force.

Also remember, Beloved, that we are part of the Earth, as well. Our physical bodies are made up of elements found within our Earth Mother. We are creations of Earth and Spirit."

Chapter 5 - Shift Your Earth-Mind

Ingrrid and I are trying a new way of communicating this morning. We formed a circle of light. We merged our consciousnesses, and our physicality is aligning the giving and receiving reception areas.

Ingrrid says...

"Let us remain merged for this session and see how it goes."

So I stand ready with my pen poised and I receive words that sounded crazy to me.

Ingrrid continues...

"Please extinguish all smoking materials."

Well heck, what am I supposed to do with that? but I wrote it down anyway and then Ingrrid pipes in and says...

"That was a test, Rebecca. We wanted to see if you would write what we expressed when it doesn't seem to make any sense. It did not make any sense and yet you wrote it. Well done.

You must be willing to write every word that comes without trying to figure it out ahead-of-time. You're very good at this and yet we desire you to move to the next level of letting go, both in your live channeling and in writing. The merging exercise will help you. Merge with me and remain merged when you're channeling in your next live event.

I can assist you in adjusting your energy each time your channel, if you desire. We have much the same mission. We are both channels of valuable, precious, life-saving information. Please write what we say even if you don't think it makes sense. It will make sense, as you will see."

And then I think, *Gee, what kind of crazy things are you going to have me write?*

On a more serious note, Ingrrid continues...

"Long ago when the Earth was recognized for the living entity that She is, peace reigned in the land. Sure, there were some small disputes over lands, properties, even cattle, yet it was a peaceful time. As technology advanced, men became more and more concerned with the living of day-to-day life with an eye always to the future.

> *"Long ago when the Earth was recognized for the living entity that She is, peace reigned in the land.*

Slowly, yet it seemed like an epidemic, for the most part, men ceased to enjoy the living in the moment.

Mankind became overly concerned with either events that happened in the past, or events that were to come. Sound familiar? Because much time and thought were focused on past events, attention was given to past grievances.

Focusing on past grievances caused the heart of man to swell with bitterness. More disputes occurred. People began to talk much of perceived offenses and tried to get others to take their side; thus an insignificant, perhaps unintended oversight, ignorance, or slight became a cause for war.

Adding to this mix, attentions became focused on what would happen in the future if these past grievances were not rectified. If no one was held accountable, then what would the future hold? Even though the neighbor or friend appeared to be living peacefully in the present, no value was given to that present moment.

Let us bring this scenario into modern times.

When someone offends us, even slightly, do we not roll it around in our minds until it becomes oversized like a giant, ice-cold, filled-with-bricks-and-sticks snowball? In contrast, we spend too much time worrying about the future and hoping to direct life the exact way we want it to go.

The secret to living a much happier life is to practice self-disciplined thinking. Most of the time, we allow thoughts to rule our emotions. This can cause a big chain of other thoughts to cascade and create blockages to happiness."

Rebecca questioning...

"Whah, boo-hoo. How do we do otherwise? I see the pattern and I am certainly guilty. I worry about the past. If a driver honks and shakes their fist at me, I play it over and over in my mind. Even though I try to let it go, it seems to still be there, disrupting my peace.

If I have an appointment on Monday, I spend the weekend worrying if I'll make it on time and what will happen. Yes, I worry about my bills; will I be able to pay them? I worry about certain habits; will I ever stop doing them? Are these habits interfering in my life or my health?

I worry about my children; will they be happy? Can I do anything to help them be happier? Then comes the worries about my grandchildren. Oh my goodness, will they be safe and happy in their lives? So, Ingrrid, I am a prime example of what you are saying.

I understand right now how our thoughts can run away with us. Do you have a solution?"

Ingrrid replies...

"Well, I could tell you to stop thinking about the past and the future, but that would be futile. You need something you can replace this habit with, for Beloved, this is only a habit and all habits can be shifted. I have an easy way to shift.

Shift your Earth mind.

Your Earth mind may not find so much pleasure in this, so it may not easily cease its constant attention to the past or future, so you are going to give a job to your subconscious mind

This is best done before sleep, but can be done during the day, as well. Here's what you say:

'Subconscious mind, there is only this moment right now.

I clear my slate of past memories of pain.

Real or imagined, I replace all pain with grace and forgiveness.

I reside in the present and bring peace here.

I cannot imagine the future, for there is only light there.

I place light in my future.'

This exercise will take some discipline in reminding yourself. Beloved, even if you are only successful in doing this once, you do great good for yourself. You do great good for the energies of the past and the energies of the future."

Rebecca speaking...

So, being ever-practical, I ask, "How can we use this advice to help with our Earth's dilemma; to help in partaking of the Earth's bounty with more respect?"

Ingrrid gives us a beautiful exercise. It's called **The Restoration Exercise:**

1. Imagine a large circle of light.

2. Call all your ancestors into the circle with you. They will come.

3. Create an altar in the circle. This is an altar to honor the living entity you call Earth.

4. Imagine placing on your altar all the transgressions against the Earth made by you or your ancestors.

5. Take responsibility; own the fact that you had some part in it. Own the fact that your ancestors played a part in it, too.

6. Kneel before the altar.

7. Ask forgiveness.

8. Acknowledge the Earth for the living creative genius that She is.

9. Send grace and acknowledgment.

10. Pledge to be aware of Her. Pledge to appreciate Her. Pledge to respect Her.

Chapter 6 - Let Us Talk of Miracles

The quickest way to advance is through appreciation of your every thought. Think and then send appreciation. Both human and Spirit beings will indeed warm themselves by your fire.

People don't understand the power of appreciation because most have never made a conscious effort to exercise it.

As you consciously and lovingly send out appreciation, you will be astonished at how your life moves forward in a positive way. Need more money? Appreciate the money you have and if you don't have any, appreciate the money someone else has. Appreciate that you are not as bad off as you could be.

When I came into my circle of light this morning, before merging with Ingrrid, I noticed a large group of people who also came to the edge of the circle. To the right was a mighty elephant. I asked what the elephant was for and Ingrrid said, "To show might coupled with gentleness."

Rebecca questioning...

"Ingrrid, can we talk about miracles? I have dreamed twice that there were miracle manifestations of anointing oil flowing from my hands during my live meetings."

Ingrrid says...

"Yes, I'm here to answer your questions on any topic. If it is in your heart, it has value to be explored. Remember that I am your teacher and I take on only one student each time. I am called by the Holy Spirit Council to be of service.

Let us talk of miracles, miracle providers and miracle receivers.

There can be no efficient miracle unless there is first a need. The need sends out signals. The Universe responds and sends the answer. Now, this is almost never the result that may be expected.

Sometimes, the miracle is in acceptance. Sometimes the miracle is in medical intervention. Sometimes the miracle is in spiritual growth caused by the original need."

Rebecca speaking...

"Wait Ingrrid, I'm getting lost here. Can you define 'miracle' as you see it? To me, miracle means some great phenomenal change like someone hopping up out of a wheelchair and shouting, 'I am healed.' What say you?"

Ingrrid replies...

"To us, all life is a miracle. Any shifting of energies for the better is a miracle. Just the fact that you took on human form and came to

46

experience life is a miracle. What you are referring to in the 'hopping up from a wheelchair' and shouting 'I am healed' is another thing.

We call that a spatial miracle occurrence. For this type of miracle to occur, key things must be set in motion. Of course, need is number one. Number two is faith and this can be of equal import; faith on the part of the receiver and faith on the part of the miracle worker.

Number three is acceptance. The one receiving the spatial miracle must accept the newness of the healing. Sometimes folks do receive miraculous healings and sadly allow themselves to slip back into the condition because they simply cannot accept the full mercies of the healing.

> *Healings and miracles are simply energies shifting. Everything is energy and energy is at your command. Learn from your brother Jesus.*

Healings and miracles are simply energies shifting. Everything is energy and energy is at your command. Learn from your brother

Jesus. He knew he was in command of all energies when he walked on water. He was in command of the energies of the elements and of his physical body.

When he calmed the storm, he was in command of the energies. When he cast spirits out of the swine, he was in command of the energies. Jesus knew he was in command. He knew he was divine, yet no more divine than you are. Why do you think Jesus did not start his public ministry until he was in his 30's?

At the age of 32, he would have been considered a very mature man in those days. The life expectancy was not as great as it is now. Jesus was learning to be a master to command energies in all those years prior to the beginning of his public ministry.

He was not born with magical powers, with this knowledge of commanding energy. He had to learn it. What kind of example would our brother Jesus have been if he was born with magical powers? Yes, he always knew he was Divine and that is the only gift he came in with.

Of course he did choose supportive parents; he did not have to contend with parental abuse. Jesus, our brother, did indeed come to show that we are all Divine; we all have access to the same powers and divinities; we are one. Why do you suppose he said, 'Greater things than this shall you do?'

48

He would have been asking you to do something impossible if let's suppose—as people do—that Jesus was born with magical miracle powers. How could he have kept them hidden for 32 years? How could he have held back healing the sick? Surely, his family and friends had many sick among them.

How could he have held back raising a few dead people here and there? He did not start to perform any miracle publicly until he was fully ready; until he was confident in his ability to command energy. Jesus spent a lot of time alone. He needed this time to grow in grace and to develop his abilities.

> *If one learns to command energy and his or her heart is not aligned properly, miracles will become entertainment and turn into a dog-and-pony show.*

He needed to learn from his own team of Holy Spirit helpers. Yes, even Jesus had to get his heart in the right place to be a steadfast bringer of light; to be wise in delivering spatial miracles Jesus performed. He had to have his heart completely lined up with the Divine Flame and Divine Guidance.

49

If one learns to command energy and his or her heart is not aligned properly, miracles will become entertainment and turn into a dog-and-pony show. Greed can manifest, and ego can get in the way. (And as a side note to me) This is one reason you are learning these mastery techniques, Rebecca, because you have been working on aligning your heart to do this for good and only for good.

Remember, there are two faith requirements in order for spatial miracles to occur: faith from the one in need and faith from the one commanding energy. As you move forward, more knowledge will be added."

Chapter 7 - The Power of Appearance and the Strength to Back It Up

"Greetings, wonderful teacher. What do you want to talk about today?" I say.

I form my circle of light and in my inner circle appeared one sumo wrestler, then two. They postured themselves and then they bumped bellies. This was to show the power of appearance.

It is important to make a powerful appearance and then have the strength to back it up. These two sumo wrestlers do both (Ingrrid knows that I get bored easily, so every morning I'm experiencing delightful things in my circle of light before we begin our dictation.).

This morning I heard Ingrrid say, "Drink your coffee. I can't work with a half-awake brain wave." So I said, "Some of my best channeling has come when I wasn't fully awake." To which Ingrrid replied, "Yes, that was rather unconscious spontaneous channeling. It was good, yet I'll show you a better way: channeling by appointment.

> "Drink your coffee. I can't work with a half-awake brain wave."

You and I have a standing appointment for at least one hour of channeling every morning at 8 AM Pacific. It is best for your mind to be awake and clear for this to be most beneficial."

Now in case some of you are thinking, 'Oh I can't believe she drinks coffee,' coffee is a bean, straight from nature, and I love it. It reminds me of my childhood and until I'm told 'by them' to give it up, I shall enjoy my beautiful two cups of fresh-ground, aroma-filled Ambrosia every morning.

Ingrrid continues...

"You see, Rebecca, in case you are not aware of this yet, you are writing a book. It is to be ready by the end of February. Oh and by the way, it's December already. We Holy Spirit Brotherhood are lining up everything necessary for it to be published."

Then I felt the energy of Enoch coming through and he said...

"I am observing these proceedings and giving streams-of-thought through Ingrrid. I just wanted to pop in and introduce myself officially and personally offer my service." Of course, I said, "Thank you, Enoch."

Enoch continues...

"We are many here to serve in this way. We hear the hearts of mankind crying and we seek to bring comfort. This book, *The Book of*

Comfort, will bring much. Each chapter can be read alone. Someone can pick up the book, ask for guidance and open to any page.

The chapters will be short, concise and easily read. The books will go into hard copy print and people will treasure them. They will highlight sentences. Some will even start study groups around them. Many will be building a temple of Holy Spirit Council.

You will be given detailed instructions on this. Of course, you will credit our wonderful Jean K. Foster for being the catalyst to these energy transferences, and so it is."

Chapter 8 - The Little-known Solution to Every Problem

This morning in my circle of light was Ingrrid and he had King Solomon with him. Outside my circle, I felt a huge crowd gathered around; the whole of humanity.

I started to meditate and felt my mind wander off thinking about Heart Point Technique; specifically about getting the information into the world in a bigger way. I gently brought myself back to focus. Ingrrid was waiting. He has the patience of a saint. Hey, maybe he is a saint.

So, I merged with Ingrrid to line up our brain physicalities. Giving and receiving information centers aligned – check. Heart centers aligned – check. When I tuned into the united beating of our hearts, they seemed to have the same rhythm, tapping out a tune actually *How can we help? How can we help? How can we help?*

"Let us begin," Ingrrid speaks.

"King Solomon wishes to address this great crowd that is gathered around. I did not have you merge with him today, Rebecca. You have already worked with King Solomon in the past and he is acclimated to your energy waves and to the way you receive energy. He was very happy to have been called upon in the past and wishes to share directly."

Rebecca...

I turn to King Solomon and ask, "What do you wish to speak about, Dear King? I am ready to share what you have to say with all those who would listen."

King Solomon speaks...

"I wish to share much of what I have learned, both as a ruler here on Earth and as a master. It was fortunate that I was humble enough to ask for the gift of wisdom. It is true that a great flow of wisdom was imparted to me by that great energy stream you refer to as Holy Spirit.

True wisdom, Beloved, is generated by the heart. True wisdom flows directly from the heart and when you have wisdom, you have the key to understanding all things."

I will share how each and every person on Earth today can also grow in wisdom. For wisdom does not depend entirely upon your brain cells. True wisdom, Beloved, is generated by the heart. True wisdom flows directly from the heart and when you have wisdom, you have the key to understanding all things."

56

Rebecca speaking...

"Solomon, thank you for giving us this prelude to building our own Holy Spirit temple. Your wisdom and guidance on this is greatly appreciated. You say the temple is only built in one's imagination. Doesn't it depend on human will to build it and on human will to visit it?" Here I stopped to pour myself a cup of coffee. My mind wandered off again.

I heard King Solomon say, "Heart-connect with me, Beloved, and let us continue."

King Solomon continues...

"It matters not whether the inner temple is visited once a day or once a week in the broad spectrum. The temple itself will remain steadfast, waiting for you whenever you're ready. It is for your benefit that you visit often.

What matters most is how quickly you want to grow in wisdom and how ready are you to grow in wisdom. When you are ready for rapid growth, you will visit often.

As Rebecca is writing these words, her mind has wandered off twice now. I say this not to chastise, but to show that it is only human nature for the mind to wander. It serves no purpose for you to feel unworthy just because your mind wanders when you are trying to meditate or do any spiritual work. We find you even more wonderful, wondrous, and uplifting when we see you struggle to focus and then bring yourself back. The important thing is that you do bring yourself back and please have mercy on yourself.

It serves no purpose for you to feel unworthy just because your mind wanders when you are trying to meditate or do any spiritual work.

Be easy with yourself. Do not give up, especially in the inner temple of Holy Spirit visitations. Determine to visit your temple often. Invite your team of Holy Spirit Council to meet with you there. Any effort is appreciated. Any effort is believable; any and all efforts are beneficial both to you and to your team of Holy Spirit advisors. Your imagination is absolutely the greatest tool there is for attaining both wisdom and spiritual growth. When you ascend upwards into your imagination, you are joining forces with spirits in charge of assisting and creation. Did you know there are guardians of thought and imagination? Let us call them the Committee of Creation.

These appointed beings monitor thoughts of humanity. They monitor for the purpose of creating solutions, for everything is created in Spirit form first and then filtered back into the hearts and minds of men. Some of these creative solutions are... guess what? Heart's desires. They are given by Spirit. In fact, every heart's desire is given by Spirit.

Here's how it works: a problem is thought upon by one or more people. If it is a huge problem, it creates a bigger picture. Beings of light monitor and begin to formulate various solutions. These solutions are then interjected gently into several who will be catalysts for implementing the solution. If the solution-bearing individual listens to the message their heart is giving them, the passion will awaken knowledge in the brain centers. Without heart's passion first, there would be no drive for a solution."

Solomon continues...

"Sometimes part of this committee will incarnate to experience more fully the problem so that they can return to the other side and work on the solution more knowledgably. The hardest job of this solution committee is getting the recipients of the solution to come to life because many times, the answer is disguised as a heart's urging. Often, beings get caught up in living and do not listen to or acknowledge their heart's yearnings.

There should be a course in every educational system of following your heart. Now, let us return to our discussion on using the imagination.

When you use the imagination for positive creation, you activate many levels of creation. When the committee who seeks to help bring solutions to mankind sees the light shining from your imagination, it brings great joy in the heavens by your intended focus of your imagination. You are assisting greatly in the creation process.

> *When you use the imagination for positive creation, you activate many levels of creation.*

The next time you visit your inner temple, allow yourself to tune into the committee. You'll notice that they rush to see if they can be of assistance.

This is one way to use visualizing more effectively. Acknowledge that you have a team of Holy Spirit helpers. Acknowledge that you have a team of the committee that is delighted to see you using your imagination to create. Begin now to use your imagination in even more detailed settings. Imagine the thing you want to create and install every detail of this creation.

Remember this: don't leave out the feeling part of your creation. How will you feel when you have manifested this creation? How will others feel? If you don't think others will be happy, leave them out of the creation process.

Now, I know that you have heard about imagination and visualization as powerful tools. This is not new. What I bring to the mixture is the knowledge I have about the Creation Committee. Now you know that as you use your imagination to create, you have assistance.

You have the Creation Committee. You also have the energetic spiritual assistance of your Holy Spirit team and Beloved Ones. You have the assistance and full support of any being of light that you conjure up in your imagination.

Rebecca speaking...

And I ask, "How?"

Solomon responds...

"Imagine that Jesus is in your temple or circle of light. Ask for his help. Imagine Raphael is in your temple or circle of light. Ask for his help. Imagine Aphrodite, Goddess of Love and Beauty is with you and guiding you.

Beloved, I have given you the keys to creation. Seek wisdom by visiting your inner temple often. If you simply wish to visit and ask for wisdom, this is a very great thing and it shall certainly be granted to you. It has been my honor to speak to you. Thank you, Rebecca, and thank you, Ingrrid."

Chapter 9 – Sometimes It's Private...

"Good morning, Ingrrid," I cheerily called out. "Thank you for switching the appointment time."

I had a restless night tossing and turning, unable to sleep soundly. At 2:30 AM when my eyes still wouldn't close, I sent a message to Ingrrid: *Can we switch our appointment time from 8 AM to 9 AM?* Having these appointments to write is not a burden to me. It is something I look forward to very much. However, I am so glad to have flexibility.

Ingrrid surprised me by saying that today's message was just for me, so I switched to my personal journal to take today's message into my heart. Ingrrid assures me that our conversation for this book will continue tomorrow.

Chapter 10 – Prelude to Building a Temple

Good morning, Ingrrid. I'm sure you were tuning into my worries. I'm also sure Mother Azna is with you now. We will discuss my worries soon. As you know, I am very, very normal and I have been going through some of my own personal angst in the last few days. I have spent the first part of the morning in meditation with my dear divine Mother Azna. Let us begin a transmission.

In my circle of light this morning, there was only Ingrrid; no visitors. We rose up into space of the great void; here was nothing but darkness and stillness. Ingrrid told me "Make your circle of light bigger. Now make it smaller. So small there is only room for one. Now make it large again. Now let us embrace. Feel my heart beating. Now merge. Unmerge. Merge sideways. Unmerge except for the feet. Now merge and stay focused on your body being merged with mine. Get the feel of what it's like to be merged with a Master."

So, I did as I was asked, but I felt nothing unusual at all in doing this exercise. No tingles; no great insights; no phenomena at all.

"Ingrrid," I asked, "was there a specific purpose to this exercise?"

"Yes," Ingrrid replied. "There was, to test you, dear Rebecca."

"Oh good Lord, again?" I asked.

"Yes, Beloved One. To test you, to see if you still hear me, still follow my guidance even though you see no purpose. We intentionally dulled your feeling receptors so that you would receive the instructions with your mind only. You felt nothing, expected nothing, yet you followed me every step of the way. You hesitated not once at each instruction. Well done, now we shall speak of things close to your heart.

You have asked me, or us, to give you a more detailed map of creation, a bird's-eye view of the heart's temple. Heart and mind together shall construct this temple of Holy Spirit dwelling and Council. To give a little history on the idea of temple building, let us bring in the greatest builder of all, Enoch the Great."

Rebecca questioned...

"Enoch? Wasn't he known for walking with God and ascending to heaven without dying?" I don't think he was remembered at all for building anything."

Ingrrid speaking...

"You are correct. He was not well-known for building physical buildings, yet his inner temple was quite extraordinary. What was unique about Enoch among other things is that he was a great master of dreams. Enoch would lay out what he wished to have guidance on, all before he slept. As he slept, he would leave his physical temple and walk in his etheric temple during his nighttime vigils.

Although his body and mind were sleeping, his soul was communicating with God. This became a habit; a nightly occurrence. He brought back many ideas and put them into practical use. He did write down much about his soul's journey, yet much of that is not understood.

Enoch sought to protect the knowledge by his vast use of symbology. If one wanted to understand, to unlock the wisdom and the keys of Enoch, he would meditate on them daily for a period of at least 10 minutes without interruption.

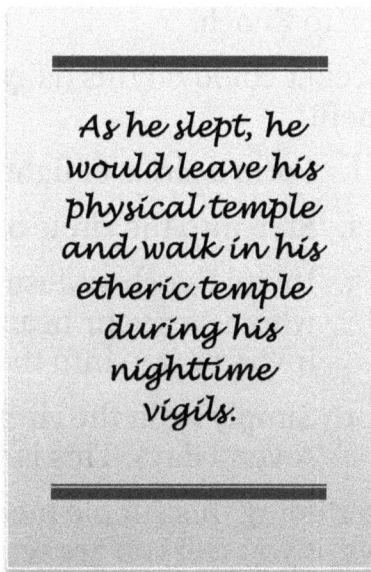

As he slept, he would leave his physical temple and walk in his etheric temple during his nighttime vigils.

Rebecca, I had you meditate and hold the merge with me for 10 full minutes to prep you to deliver this message. You felt nothing while merging with me, correct?"

Rebecca speaking...

"Nothing," I replied. "No tingle, no insights, just wondering why in the world you were doing this."

Ingrrid continues....

"So Rebecca, if you feel nothing and yet you comply with your guide's instructions, you set an example of faith to others. Now let us get back to Enoch.

A seeker could do this daily exercise with great benefit:

1. Form a circle of light.

2. Step into the circle of light yourself.

3. Invite Enoch or Jesus or Mary or whomever your heart felt guided to invite to step into the circle with you.

4. Simply be in the circle with them for several days. This is your test of faith.

After doing this simple meditation for several days, if you feel you are ready, merge with the other being. Line up your physicalities; line up your heart; line up your minds. Do this even though you feel nothing. Do not be waiting to feel anything.

This is what we call blind faith. When you "try on" blind faith, you show great potential in becoming a spiritual master. It is a very immature spirit that must have instant proof that they are receiving inner guidance. For the master-in-training to become a leader in the Golden Age, many tests of blind faith will be presented."

> *This is what we call blind faith. When you "try on" blind faith, you show great potential in becoming a spiritual master.*

Rebecca speaking...

"Time for me to step in. Ingrrid, this is good information and I feel we're getting a bit off topic here. We started by talking about Enoch and got way over into this blind faith business."

Ingrrid replies...

"I was getting to the point by laying a foundation for all to clearly understand. Enoch was a great builder of a faith temple. He will now guide us in building a temple of Inner Light.

Divine Mother is having her input in this as well as all your spirit team. It is important, Rebecca, to give credit to one who opened this portal of understanding about the Holy Spirit being more than an energy stream. It was revealed to Jean K. Foster as she wrote in *The God-Mind Connection*, the Holy Spirit is also a team of God's helpers."

Ingrrid continues...

"The brotherhood of Holy Spirit consists of both male and female masters, angels, and those you may consider deities. To be in the brotherhood of Holy Spirit is a great honor and only the very elect shall be appointed. Each member has the option to serve the equivalent of five earth years and then may petition to continue or be assigned to another mission.

When you accept the indwelling of Holy Spirit and then construct a thought temple for their presence, your spirit life will catapult in mighty leaps forward. You will construct an inner temple to Holy Spirit, yet you can do so much within this temple.

Visit here daily and you will be amazed at how you grow. Bring all your problems here to be addressed by Holy Spirit Council. Now, allow us to guide you in creating your own temple."

Chapter 11 - Temple Building 101

Yesterday I fully intended to come back, do another meditation and get the full scope of temple-building, but guess what? Life happens and I simply did not have the time. But, I'm here now and this is our regular committed appointment time.

This morning I had a hard time staying focused on the circle of light. Ingrrid was there, as well as Enoch.

Yesterday we started to talk about building a temple for Holy Spirit Council and it is time to finish it up today. So, finding it hard to concentrate, I keep pulling my mind back from its wanderings. Ahh, I left the circle of light and went to visit my own temple. Yes, of course. I have constructed my own temple to communicate with my Holy Spirit Council.

Let me tell you about my temple.

The outer sanctuary that I built for practice sessions is now huge; so huge in fact that I have to use a motorized cycle to get to the front. I constructed this part of my temple to practice new techniques, new teachings, and other new things that I want to do in front of a spirit audience. Whenever I want to try out a new gift, I come here first to practice in spirit.

Next, I visited my hospital. This is a new concept in healing. When someone asks me for prayer for a physical healing, I bring them here and construct a special room in my hospital just for them. I fix it up like I feel they would like it. It's more like a spa room than a hospital room.

Then, I invite the healing masters to come and work with their bodies and spirits. When I think of my "patients" I simply send light. It is no longer my responsibility to try and heal them. It is up to their own spirit and the healing masters.

For today, I constructed a new room in my own temple; a room for finance and business advice. I invited experts in all phases of finances and business together here to work on my business with me.

Finally, I went into my own spa room to relax and refresh myself. Now, after my little visit to the temple, I'm ready to return to the circle of light and see what Ingrrid and Enoch have for today.

Patiently, Ingrrid and Enoch were waiting for me in the circle of light. This time there was a beautiful angelic choir. They were singing in beautiful harmony; singing of my heart's desires; praising my heart's desires, for they know that the beautification of man is found only by experiencing the heart's deepest desires.

So, I said to Enoch, great builder of faith, one who walks with God, "Will you give us guidance on constructing a mind temple, a thought temple, as a dwelling place of Holy Spirit?"

Enoch replies...

"Yes, I am very happy to give some guidelines. Every person must construct and change their own temple to please themselves, yet there are some essentials that make for a good inner temple.

First, get into the space of being comfortable and relaxed. Create a circle of light. Realize that you do indeed have a team of Holy Spirit helpers just waiting to be asked to join up with you. Make your circle of light larger and invite your own personal team of Holy Spirit helpers to step into the circle with you. Acknowledge them. Just be in the circle of light with them for a bit.

Tell your group of Holy Spirit helpers that you require their assistance in constructing a temple for them to assist you and advise you. Imagine what kind of setting you want your temple to be in. Would you like it to be at the beach? the mountains? the forest? the plains? perhaps a combination of several? Whatever you desire, Beloved. Your setting is yours to choose.

Today is only the bare minimum of construction. You may add to it each time you visit, if you wish. Construct a beautiful room.

Add gold, silver, jewels, polished wood, flowers, beautiful tapestries, draperies, whatever your heart desires, for this first room should be to honor your heart's desires. Construct an altar; as ornate as you wish. Imagine all your heart's desires are piled up there. They are so very important; so sacred are these heart's desires. Two angels stand at each end of your altar. So precious are your heart's desires that these angels guard your sacred altar night and day.

Now comes a choir of angels singing praises to your heart's desires. The sound is lovely and you feel so encouraged. Construct a beautiful choir loft so they have their own special place to sing praises about your heart's desires. Visit this room often.

> Now comes a choir of angels singing praises to your heart's desires. The sound is lovely and you feel so encouraged.

Next, you will construct a special room for meeting with and receiving counsel from your Holy Spirit team. Construct it well. You may expand this room as you desire. Sometimes when you return, you will find your

Holy Spirit Council has been decorating to make it even more lovely.

For today, imagine your team of Holy Spirit helpers is here. They are so grateful that you have acknowledged them. Send them appreciation. As often as you return to this temple is how much you will grow spiritually.

It takes blind faith to construct a temple and to believe that you have your own team of Holy Spirit helpers. Blind faith is the very best kind of faith. It leads you into very deep, precious, spiritual waters.

Remember, the most important two rooms to begin with are:

1. the room to house the altar of your heart's desires, and

2. a Council room for you to meet and get advice from your Holy Spirit helpers

The next phase of your building project can be as follows:

Build an etheric hospital on your temple grounds. When someone asks you for prayer for physical ailments, bring their spirit here. Ask the ascended masters who specialize in healing to work with them here. Once you place them in your hospital setting and give their care over to the etheric healers... let it go. When you do think of them, do not do so with frantic worry. Send light to their spirit. Send appreciation to the team of healers. If their spirit is willing to get better, this is all that is needed.

Please take time each day to visit your temple. You will be in wonder at the insight you get from your team of Holy Spirit helpers. Your team has been waiting to be acknowledged. They desire to help you with all things in your life and especially, Beloved, to realize your heart's desires, for your heart's desires are the most important treasures and you came to Earth to manifest those desires."

Later that day...

Rebecca speaking...

"Ingrrid, "I missed your assistance when connecting with Enoch this morning. It was a bit harder to interpret the thoughts of Enoch. The energy was different, with longer pauses between words."

Ingrrid replies...

"All is as it should be, Rebecca. I am like an interpreter for you. With Enoch, I just stepped back and let you do it. You did well, Rebecca. We love how you just do it anyway, even if you feel it's not perfect.

You did well, Rebecca. We love how you just do it anyway, even if you feel it's not perfect.

If you allow me to be of more assistance, I can amplify the stream from Sanat Kumara, Jesus, or anyone you desire to communicate with, as well as our Beloved Mother Azna.

We are all delighted to offer our services. Did you know that your own Council called me in as a candidate to be of great help to you in your channeling? I'm not greedy for recognition. Simply give me the word to help you express any entity and I will do so. Think of me as a sound-mixing machine; many sounds come into the mixer and emerge as a harmonious chorus that delights the listeners."

Rebecca speaking...

"Okay, Ingrrid. You have my permission to assist me. Can you help me more powerfully embody the angelic being, deity, or ascended master that I am channeling?"

"Yes," Ingrrid replied. "Absolutely, and your energy will never feel tired. Afterwards, you will be exhilarated and refreshed. Okay, done.

Anyone who channels multiple entities such as you do can ask for someone on his or her Holy Spirit team to be called in as an interpreter to make connection easier. Holy Spirit Council will choose someone very close to them in energy patterns, yet with great understanding. No one need even know that there is a helper there. It will simply flow smoother with increased accuracy."

Rebecca speaking...

"Ingrrid, have we discussed enough of my personal responsibilities for this phase of my life?"

Ingrrid replies...

"Let us become clear together. You are to receive words of wisdom and express them with great vigor, knowing that the words you bring are indeed healing, uplifting, truth, and the lifeblood of what thriving in the New Age must be."

Rebecca speaking...

"You know what, Ingrrid? I feel just a little bit crazy sometimes, like something is happening to me or through me. I feel different, like old things are not as important to me. Earth things are not as important. Sometimes, okay... much of the time, I wake up in the night to check the time because I'm so eager for our appointment. This receiving has taken on utmost importance to me."

Ingrrid replies...

"It is simply time, Rebecca. Time for a stepping-up of information that will help those who can hear. This is your heart's longing to receive and share these messages. Your head may feel a little crazy, as you say, for your head is not so accustomed to being over-run by the heart.

> Your head may feel a little crazy, as you say, for your head is not so accustomed to being over-run by the heart.

The teachings you bring are a great help to the hearts of others. You are a wondrous one for awakening the heart centers—the truth centers—by delivering these messages as given to you by Spirit."

Chapter 12 - How to Get Your Own 'Teaching Angels'

Again, I asked for a later appointment time. I gave a wonderful party last night for all my friends that I go dancing with. When I saw that my guests were enjoying themselves so much and lingering quite late, I gave myself some grace and asked for a later appointment time. I always want to come to our meeting well-rested and ready to receive. *So what shall we speak of today, dear Ingrrid?*

This morning in my circle of light, there appeared Ingrrid. With him were three beautiful angels. Ingrrid explained that these were special teaching angels. These angels are here to teach me more about how thought can manifest into the physical world.

I get the sensation that they will spend some time simply observing me to see how much I know already. They are giving me a slight correction on that last sentence. They will be observing how much of my heart I am using in my own thought-creating. Very interesting.

I am delighted to work with these three teaching angels to learn more about how thoughts manifest. You, the reader, will come along and have the great benefit of learning through my writing. You as reader may be curious to know how I receive communication from this group of angels because there are three. How do I hear them? Yes, there are three, yet they function as one. I sense they are conferring among themselves and then I get a sensation of thought. Why are there three?

It seems each one of the three has their simple way of teaching as a specialty. These angels were chosen by my Holy Spirit team because they petitioned for the job and also because they love sharing their knowledge with Rebecca. Hearing this piqued my curiosity.

Rebecca speaking...

I asked, "Ingrrid, why did these three teaching angels petition to be assigned to me?"

Ingrrid answers...

"Because they have heard the messages you've given about following your heart. They see you teaching Heart Point Technique which acknowledges the wisdom of the heart.

These angels know that as they teach you, you will teach others. The groundwork, the very foundation of what is needed, this knowing the importance of the heart is already in place. That is why they petitioned to be assigned to you."

Rebecca speaking...

With Ingrrid's energy in place beside me, I can easily tune into the group. So, you the reader may be asking, "How can I get my own

Ingrrid? How can I learn the same way you are learning?"

"Anyone can learn and do the same way that I learn and do. Start by tuning into your heart. Ask yourself why you have this longing. Let that be the #1 reason you want to learn more; to satisfy your heart's longing. Then peruse the teachings in this book to see if they feel true to your heart. If you feel no truth here, put down this book at once and seek the path your heart calls you toward.

If you feel the truth of this book lines up with your heart, then create your own inner temple, if you haven't already. Invite the presence of Holy Spirit to manifest in your life daily. Do the Flame-On exercise by Sanat Kumara, the great ascended master and keeper of the Holy Flame.

Let that be the #1 reason you want to learn more; to satisfy your heart's longing.

Visit your inner temple daily and seek the counsel of your Holy Spirit team. Do this faithfully with no thought of phenomena.

Whether you feel anything or not, wisdom shall surely come.

There is great merit and opportunity for advancement by putting this visit to your inner temple as a most important aspect of your day. If you are really hungry for truth and spiritual growth, make this a daily appointment. Let nothing keep you away from your appointment.

If you cannot make the appointed preset time, send an energetic request to have the appointment shifted to a more appropriate time and then keep that appointment. There is so much benefit in making a commitment and keeping a commitment. Nothing great really happens until there is a sincere commitment.

Before going on to the next chapter, take time to review what has been presented so far. If you have not created your inner temple, then go back and do so. Do not move forward in this book until you know your heart is ready.

Just because you feel a bit nervous or even a lot nervous doesn't mean you cannot go forward on this path.

Just because you feel a bit nervous or even a lot nervous doesn't mean you cannot go forward on this path. The

84

writings in this book may have stirred up some old beliefs and doubts within you. There are many erroneous teachings of churches, teachers, and cultures that have kept you in energetic shackles.

Some of these beliefs and teachings may have embedded themselves in your heart. Take these feelings into your temple and ask your Holy Spirit team to give you guidance. Once you are feeling clear, proceed with the next chapter."

Chapter 13 - Rudimentary Steps to Manifesting With Thought

So eager was I to explore this information on manifesting with thought energy, that I asked for another appointment the same day. I made myself another cup of coffee, ate a few bites of yogurt and I was ready.

I began by creating a circle of light; the three teaching angels were already there. Ingrrid was there also. He seemed very relaxed; more like an observer.

The three teaching angels, hmmm, let's give this group a name. They signaled by thought. Teachers of Thought, T.O.T. for short. Short and simple. I like it. T.O.T.

The T.O.T. group still seemed to be assessing my receiving receptors to determine the very best way to transfer information. They suggested I take a moment and run light through my body.

You may want to pause and read the instructions to do this, too. I suggest that you read the entire instructions and then do the exercise.

1. Focus on the divine flame within your heart.

2. Bring it up to wear like a crown; tongues of fire above your head.

3. Ask for Holy Spirit revelation light to gather in your higher self-point; 18-24" above your head.

4. Bring down this light through the crown, the corpus callosum, the hypothalamus, back to the pineal, forward to the pituitary, down through all the acupressure meridian points around your eyes.

5. Finally, stream the light down through the heart. Put your focus on your physical beating heart as you imagine light of Holy Spirit revelation touching on what is needed for this segment.

This is simple yet powerful. Don't expect to feel anything. It matters not whether you feel anything or not. This is a positive, prime example of blind faith and as we have discussed earlier, blind faith is the very best kind to practice.

> *It matters not whether you feel anything or not. This is a positive, prime example of blind faith and as we have discussed earlier, blind faith is the very best kind to practice.*

88

The T.O.T. group began...

"Rebecca, we're here to give you the very rudimentary steps to manifesting with thought. To explain fully is not possible in one book, yet to give the very basics of understanding is possible."

Rebecca speaking...

"We have all heard that thoughts are things; it's pretty much old news by most seekers and students of any spiritual path. What's different about what you will teach?"

The angels respond...

"Yes, we agree that you already think you know that thoughts are things. You feel you know this with your head, correct? Yet most do not truly know this in the depths of their hearts. Here is truth:

Hear it with your head and ask that it be integrated into your heart.

It is the heart integration process that is missing. When you think a thought – a thought of something you are trying to create with positive intent – the timing is absolutely instant; the thing is instantly created in spirit with no waiting.

Example: When you did the temple-building exercise on blind faith, the temple was instantly created in your thought space. It was created in etheric space. Your temple was very literally created as a dwelling place for your Holy Spirit team and for all purposes of spiritual growth. Your temple is right now created and waiting for you in this dimension."

Rebecca questions...

"What do you mean by 'this dimension'?"

T.O.T. answers...

"We mean the other side; what you refer to as heaven; the dimension you will cross into when you leave your physical bodies behind."

Rebecca questions...

"So, as we create our temple on purpose with positive intent, this is being manifested into physical form on the other side?"

T.O.T. answers...

"Yes, absolutely, and it is held in place by your continued attention to it. The only way your temple can be diminished is if you never think of it or visit it again. Then the temple would slowly fade into space. The amount of attention or focus you give to anything determines how quickly it manifests into your earthly form."

Rebecca questions...

"Wait. I have heard that if you make a request and then constantly worry and nag about it,

90

this action slows the process of manifestation. It seems that you're telling us to create it in thought and then keep giving it attention."

T.O.T. answers...

"A very good question. So glad you asked. We are speaking of two different energy streams of thought here. The energy needed to create a positive thing, sustain it with good focus is not the same as worry energy. Worry energy is noticing what you were trying to manifest is not yet here. Creating something in thought and then nagging and worrying about the time it's taking to manifest is futile to your manifesting efforts.

Here is an example of a positive way of using thought manifestation. Let's say you want something tangible like a new car. Go into your temple, present your idea of a new car to your team of Holy Spirit helpers. If your heart wants it, your team wants you to have it. They want to help you get it.

You're going to create this in thought first, correct? As you create this in thought, it will come into physical form in the etheric realm. Think about it: how can something come into physical form in the etheric realm if you are wishy-washy about it?

Pay attention here, for we are speaking about you and your deliberate intent to create a very specific thing. Be very specific in your thought creation. The basics of car-creating 101, here are some ideas:

- Would you like a new or used car?

- What is the color, make and model?

- Clarify every detail. How does it smell? How does it feel? How does it drive?

The idea here is to have fun with your creation. If you're not specific, we don't know how to help you. As you visit your team daily, let yourself have fun sitting in, admiring, and driving your creation. Ask your Holy Spirit team for help with any obstacles that prevent the car from coming to you in manifested, physical form.

Now, we think you may need some guidance in what to watch for. There are thoughts that can and certainly will delay your manifestation into physical form:

- Avoid giving thought space to thoughts such as 'How will I pay for this car?' Replace that thought with 'This car comes to me with ease.'

- Avoid thoughts of 'Others may be envious of such a fine car.' Replace that thought with 'My happiness inspires others as I drive my new car.'

- Avoid thoughts of the drawbacks of car ownership such as 'I worry about dings in the parking lot.' Replace it with 'My car is protected at all times.'

- Avoid worrying about the cost of fuel. Replace it with, 'I fuel my car with ease."

- Avoid worrying about insurance requirements. Replace it with, 'My car has the best insurance available at a great rate.'

Think of it like this. Every time you come into your manifestation space with joy, and have fun in your new car, it's forming molecule-by-molecule in your physical reality. If you allow the worry thoughts to creep in, it destroys molecule-by-molecule what you have built. This is why it is of utmost importance to guard your thoughts.

Rebecca has certainly shown you examples of her mind wandering off in the writing of this book. This is one reason we had her be so open with you about her experiences. When your mind wanders... and it will... gently bring yourself back.

Remember that your Holy Spirit team is so willing to help you. If you move quickly into self-forgiveness and self-mercy, this will override any and all damage you have done to your manifesting. So, be merciful to yourself and practice, practice, practice.

One of the great differences between your dimension and this dimension is instant manifestation. Here, if you want to go someplace, you simply think of it with clarity and you are there. Your dimension is far more dense, so it takes more effort on your part.

If you feel that this type of manifestation requires too much effort, be easy on yourself. When you get here on this side – and you most assuredly will one day – you will learn very quickly about the ease of manifesting instantly.

Here on this side, manifestation is not a talent. Here, it's just the way energy works. If you create something here that you don't entirely love, you can simply uncreate it or change it instantly to suit you. In your dimension, you need the protective barrier of time, for you have not yet learned a quick process of uncreating or changing-to-suit."

Rebecca comments...

"Hey, I thought you said earlier that when we are trying to create or manifest and allow worry thoughts to creep in, that our molecules of creation begin to dissipate.

T.O.T. responds:

"Yes, we did say that; you are indeed correct; however, we were speaking of something you were in the process of creating. In this case, we are speaking of something you already created. Let's say, if you were not diligent in the details of the car, you might bring a car into your physical space and leave out something very important like a smooth-running engine. You would still have the barrier of time to manifest that much-needed engine."

Rebecca questions...

"This causes me to ask for more guidance. If I am practicing the art of creation and manifesting, how can I be sure I am not leaving out any important details, like a smooth-running engine for my car?"

T.O.T. answers:

"In your creation, in your imagination, take the car for a test-drive. Note the way the seat fits you. Note the way the engine purrs. Note the way others look at your car in admiration. How do you feel during your test-drive? Is the color you have chosen pleasing? If not, change it. You can even ask for guidance from your Holy Spirit team, 'Hey did I leave anything out?'"

Rebecca questions...

"Can you give us a timeframe for manifesting something like a car? Seems like all of this thought energy could be a lot of work."

T.O.T. answers:

Well, you're going to be thinking something anyway. You might as well use your thoughts to create something you want! Yes, this will take some discipline. The question is: do you want to drift along in life not directing where you go or do you want to partake, influence, and enjoy the navigation process? Either way, you will surely be creating something.

Now about the timeframe: if you are diligent and protect your thoughts from worry-invasion, this could happen so fast, it would seem instantaneous. How creative can you get? Here are some ideas to help you:

* Send one or more of your Holy Spirit team to car lots, looking for the perfect vehicle for you.

* Now, if you don't feel worthy yet to be asking your team for this type of help, then go back to square one. Your car manifestation will have to wait.

*Ask for guidance from your team. Ask for anything you need to add to your creation.

* Make a vision board. Cut out pictures of your perfect car from magazines, brochures, and the newspaper. You can even include pictures of ways you want to feel while driving your car."

Rebecca questions...

"Okay, wait a minute. A red flag just went up for me when you said, 'Send one or more of your team out to car lots to look for you.' A lot of folks are going to think this is a very self-serving job to give to beings of status, such as a master of Holy Spirit. We know that our team is comprised of masters, angels, and high beings of light. Now you are saying to give one or more of them the job of going car-shopping for me?"

T.O.T. answers:

"When your particular team of Holy Spirit helpers was assigned to you, your needs, personality, and heart's desires were of utmost importance. Don't you think that if you desire a car, that a car enthusiast would be included on your team? Not only is this so, but specialists of every type are continually called in for consultations.

Do you think that life on the other side is boring? That we sit around and play harps all day only focusing on being spiritual? No! Many interests are held on this side. We continue to explore on this side.

Things that brought us joy on Earth can bring us more joy on this side. Allow us to experience utmost job satisfaction by helping you to manifest that which your heart inspires.

Now, if you're still feeling stuck, go back and review before moving forward. Go to your temple, present your questions to your team, and let the questions percolate. Be tender and merciful to yourself.

Acknowledge your doubts. How else can you address them? Sweep nothing under the rug. You can't hide your energy anyway.

Love yourself and allow us to fully love and assist you, for Beloved, it gives us great pleasure to do this. You and your growth are part of our soul's journey; we delight in your progress.

There is never any judgment when you falter; we admire you very much for any effort. We admire your quest for learning, simply by reading this book. Soon we will speak on something very dear to this writer's heart, using this manifestation process for developing deeper spiritual gifts and talents into the physical."

Appendix

Basic Heart Point Technique (HPT)

(Get the entire Heart Point Technique manual, including detailed images FREE at www.HPTFREE.com)

Description

HPT is a healing method sent from the Divine Feminine. HPT accesses the deepest wisdom of the heart and teaches soul mastery. HPT flows light energy through various acupressure meridians, organs, and glands. HPT is a spiritual/energetic healing modality.

Treatment with HPT consists of "running light" through treatment points beginning with:

- **Higher self point** (18-24 inches above head)

- **Crown point** (through corpus callosum, pineal gland, hypothalamus)

- **Third eye**, **beginning of eyebrow**, **side of eye**, **2 points just above the tear duct** and **under eye** [These are the points your hand is covering: third eye (inner vision), beginning of eyebrow (sadness), side of eye (anger), under eye (fear), inside corner of eye 1/8 inch above tear duct (site where all acupressure points enter the brain).]

- **Heart point** (just to left of center of chest)

- **Consolidation point** at nape of neck (this is used AFTER intensity is lowered) to 'tap in' a positive keyword

Step 1. Set intention of what to work on (make sure client understands all the treatment points).

Step 2. Get an intensity rating–if this applies–from 1 to 10 (1 is low; 10 is high). As the practitioner, write down this number, as well as the condition or emotion.

Step 3. If this is an emotion, ask where they feel it in their body. Ask: if this emotion had a voice, what kind of energy would it need to feel better?

Step 4. Simply accept the emotion or condition without judgment. Hold it up the light for healing as you begin to run light through the HPT points.

Step 5. Put your awareness on the higher-self point, call in light, imagine the light overflowing down into the crown, through all the points and resting in the wisdom of the heart.

If a certain energy was requested to make it feel better, interchange that name with the ancient Arabic phrase 'An Nur,'(pronounced Ahn Noor) e.g.

if client said the energy of 'acceptance' was needed, use 'An Nur' and 'acceptance' alternately. This is optional.

Because An Nur is incorruptible and self-adjusting, it can be used alone or with other words.

Tell your client to relax and simply pay attention to what comes up.

Step 6. Chant 'An Nur' on behalf of your client. It is good if they chant with you. I usually start with 27 times but you will 'get' a number in your head. It can be less or more but should be at least 7 times.

Step 7. Check back in with client and ask them to take another intensity rating between 1 and 10. It should have gone down. Sometimes, it changes to a different emotion or condition.

Proceed to work on that one emotion the same way. The key here is to simply accept whatever comes up and send light mercy and the chant to that... no judgment.

HPT Tapping

In some cases, action is required. You can tap on the HPT points, repeating the issues.

For instance, if you feel angry, tap the HPT points, simply stating the emotion you feel.

First, tune into the emotion holding HPT and get an intensity rating on a scale of 1-10.

Tapping at the crown: "I feel angry."

Third eye: "I feel angry."

Beginning of eye: "I feel angry."

Side of the eye: "I feel angry."

Under the eye: "I feel angry."

Inner eye points: "I feel angry."

Heart point: "I feel angry,"

Feel free to add any other words that express your anger, e.g. "That rotten scalawag makes me so angry!" It really helps to intensify the release if you allow yourself to fully get into the emotions of a little child when expressing any deep emotion.

When the intensity is way down, tap in a positive keyword (how do you want to feel instead) at the consolidation point at the back of the head.

Additions to Make HPT Even More Effective

Pranic tube breathing: the pranic tube runs from the perineum up to the top of the head. Breathing this way causes balance to be restored.

How to do Pranic Tube Breathing: Imagine you are breathing the energies of the earth up through the perineum and into the heart center. Imagine breathing the energies of the heavens down from the crown and into the heart. Realize this energy is always flowing.

Sound: Make the sound of the emotion. According to The Hathors (advanced beings channeled by Tom Kenyon) every emotion has a sound signature. By getting in touch with the emotion–allowing whatever primal sound we could imagine to come out–we allow it to be transmuted.

Sacred Arabic Chants: Chanting these phrases into the emotion/condition brings relief and healing. (see examples below)

Movement: If the emotion could move, what kind of movement would it be?

Helpful to ask: (holding HPT points) What kind of energy is needed to heal this?

Flame-On Exercise

This exercise was given to us by the great Ascended Master, Sanat Kumara.

I am Sanat Kumara, keeper of the Holy Flame. And I come to you with a message of great truth; the Holy Spirit is indeed part of each and every one of you as you realize what you can do with this great stream of energy. Your life will be transformed; your lives will be enhanced.

Rebecca lovingly calls this exercise, "Flame-On." This is to teach you to recognize that you are no longer a tiny little spark of divinity, you never were. It was only the falsehoods of man who drifted off into believing that they could only hold the tiniest little spark. And I say to you as keeper of that Holy Flame, keeper for many, many centuries now, that you have within you the capacity to be a roaring flame of divine light.

To do the exercise properly, focus on your heart center and imagine a spark of Divine Flame there. If an image of a tiny little flame flickers there, forgive yourself for that. This is old teaching; you're not to be blamed, beloved.

Now imagine that that flame ignites into beautiful colored flame, gold, pink, orange; many colors are in this flame. This flame enhances the God particles within every cell of your being. Next, imagine, Beloved, that you send that flame up to wear as a crown of flames above your head as on the day of Pentecost.

You know many times we have used the element of fire for a symbol of power. It was that element of fire that brought survival to the earliest man. Fire is so much more than what you believe, fire is consciousness and fire is the symbol of the Holy Spirit, of the indwelling of the Holy Spirit.

And when you realize exactly what the Holy Spirit is, you will rejoice and you will be so happy to do this exercise daily. For Beloveds, when you "flame-on" as Rebecca says, you signify to the whole creation that you know...that you know, Beloveds, that you are divine.

That you are a living embodiment of source energy of Mother-Father God, of all things Holy, you are a living embodiment. That angels and deities and saints and ascended masters see through the etheric realm and they see you with your flame and they say, "There is one who knows. Let us go and see if we can be of assistance. Let us warm ourselves by the fire of that great source."

This is the beginning of a new life for you, new sources of creation, for Beloveds, Holy Spirit power is more than what you have thought. It comes as a stream of pure energy and it is available to every man, woman, boy, and girl. You are born with that source energy within you. It cannot be otherwise. Otherwise, you would not have life. And yes, your breath enhances that flame and you can just imagine you're breathing and shooting your flames higher and we of the etheric realms say, "Yes, they understand."

It does not matter if you can't see it with your eyes, because we see it. And this is where faith comes in Beloved; we like to call it 'blind faith'. If you would hear these words, pass them through the portal of your heart and say, "Is this truth? Do I feel the truth of this divinity within me?" And if so, Beloved, do the exercise whether you see anything or not, whether you feel any tingles, whether you feel any phenomenon. Blessed is he who acts in faith, blessed is he who believes although he has not seen, blessed is he who uses the barometer of his heart.

Holy Spirit is the perfect lubricant to prayer.

You have the perfect barometer within you. And Beloved, I don't care what you feel you've done, I don't care how you've feel you messed up, you are divine, you can do this exercise. You are signifying that you believe, even if you don't quite believe. Do it and see what changes.

More on Holy Spirit

Now back to this musing on the Holy Spirit. The Holy Spirit is more than just an energy stream. If you acknowledge the Holy Spirit, it comes with a whole team of the very elect, the very elect ascended masters, angels, specialists of all types, actually petition...petition to be part of the Holy Spirit. That which is named Holy Spirit, is the highest level you could hope to attain in the evolutionary sphere. Being appointed to the realm of Holy Spirit is something that only masters can aspire to.

And if you would this day, acknowledge the end dwelling of Holy Spirit. If you will, make use of this team whose only desire is to help you move closer to that source that you already are. To help you realize you have

If you acknowledge the Holy Spirit, it comes with a whole team of the very elect, the very elect ascended masters, angels, specialists of all types, actually petition...petition to be part of the Holy Spirit.

more power than you could ever know and to help you realize Beloveds, the importance of your hearts' desires.

For now, I encourage you, believe these words, believe that you have that Holy Flame within your heart, believe you can wear it as a crown, believe that the entities, the deities, the high beings of light see you and recognize. Oh, they know they are divine, also this is a great protection from some chaotic energies, this can be a mighty protection to you. I am Sanat Kumara, keeper of the Holy Flame.

These teachings are meant to stir up questions within you, meant to bring them to the surface and I ask you to bring those questions to your Holy Spirit team if you decide to accept this teaching and you decide to allow your life to move into a new ease. That is what the Holy Spirit team does.

A Message for All from Ingrrid

Please allow your heart to be opened and ask for guidance, ask for guidance.

Ask for your own truth to become clear for you...for each of you have your own truth. There is not one truth that would fit exactly of the heart of another. Because you came here with your own plan, you came here with your own guidance; you came here to learn to experience, to grow. And you came here with the truth within your heart and with the hope that you would thrive and that you would find that God truth within you.

This is why you came forth, beloved, to learn how to express yourself, to express your heart's desire, to find that communion with source. You know you stay here such a short time compared to how long you are on the other side, it's like you're gone five minutes and you're back. But here of course, your life circumstances become so important to you that sometimes you forget the things of Spirit.

Now what's important is to honor your body and honor the things of Spirit equally. When you get out of balance is when you honor only the Spirit and do all kinds of sacrificing things with your body that are not necessary and not a sacrifice. To whom is it a sacrifice? The source energy within you?

And then sometimes we think so much of the body and only earthly things that we have no time for Spirit. And I say to you there is a very pleasant balance. There is a balance to be had and the answer, as Rebecca always says, is within your own heart. Within your own heart.

Just to tell you a little bit, of what I do for Rebecca, I am assigned to be her teacher right now. I help make the passage of information to her easier; she is to write books that will enlighten and uplift spirits and to do this it needs to be a clearing and an ease of communication, which is what I am preparing and assisting her with. I speak only to Rebecca, for I take only one student at a time, but you may have your own teacher if you accept this advice about the Holy Spirit Council. If you accept that and start to experience it... you shall know wonderful, great things. I am pleased to be of service.

Pink Net Technique

So the first angel says to the second angel, "Where did you get that awesome Merit Badge."

The second angel answers, "Oh, I got it from this really awakened human."

Angel Merit Badges? Do you think that is silly?

Here's what happened...

A friend was telling me that his boss was being so mean to him that he was about to explode (and maybe get fired). My friend felt so weak from the assault of meanness that he did not have the strength to do the Pink Net Technique himself... so I did it for him.

For this case, I used my psychic abilities to ask his (the mean boss's) angel's permission. The three spirits that walked closest to him were from the dark side. His meanness had attracted them and they were parasitically 'feasting' on his constant negativity.

I asked the three darker energies if they wanted a 'pink net of love light.' They were surprised, shocked actually, yet very eager to receive. I quickly created, then hurled a net for each one of them and they were delighted that someone had sent them a 'net of pink love light.'

With the mischievous energies distracted... (and absorbing some of that light) I was then able to work on the 'mean boss man' (BTW... I'm starting to feel bad about calling him 'mean'). I was guided to create a mini-net for each section of his brain. His seeming meanness was coming from a very imbalanced brain. Of course, I also hurled a big net over his entire energy field.

I checked back in with my friend the next day and he said, "Rebecca, I owe you profound thanks, I haven't heard a negative word or look from my boss since we talked!"

Hurray for Pink Nets of Love and Light...

So, how does this apply to angels and spirits and Merit Badges?

My guides say...

"It is time for humans to 'wake up' and realize they were given dominion over all things. When humanity realizes the tremendous power they have to 'bless,' it will be a great day indeed. By blessing your angels, guides, and spirits... you are leaping ahead in spiritual evolution! This is a sign humanity is truly ready to move into the next Golden Age."

My guides continue...

"Ask people to create these 'nets of light'-- call the name of the angel or spirit, then hurl the net with blessing. These nets will be displayed like a 'merit badge' and all the Universe will rejoice."

Every angel, spirit, energy form, you send a net to, will be proudly displaying their 'merit badges' all over the heavens. This will translate into all dimensions and levels of creation. (I think they are having a contest to see who can get the most 'merit badges'.)

Why?

Because every single 'merit badge' is a sign that another human has awakened.

Yes, this is a sign that you realize you do indeed have the power to bless the spirit world. They crave our blessings and this is just so cotton-pickin' wonderful I want to shout it from the rooftops!

Here's how you do it:

1. Intention: Whom do you want to bless with your net of pink and gold love light?

2. Creation: Create a pink net, intertwine it with gold filaments (do this with your imagination – the most potent creation tool in the Universe)

3. Hurl the net with blessings and good intent over the angel, person, or situation.

That's it. You can create these nets in an instant and create as many as you like. You can even do it for yourself.

Since getting this guidance I have created and sent nets to:

- My dog Sparky who was hit by a car
- My mom and dad who have crossed over
- All my angels and guides (and all the archangels)
- Saints
- Mother Teresa
- Azna Sophia
- Every time I think of a spirit, I create and send a net... What fun!

Questions about This Exercise

Q. 1.   How many times can I bless my angels?

   A. As often as you like. They love it.

Q. 2.   What if I don't know the names of my
         angels?

   A. Just say, "All my guardian angels,
       this is for you." (Create several
       nets because you have several
       angels.)

Q. 3.   Is there any danger of 'unwanted energy
         connection'?

   A. No, because you are hurling the
       net and disconnecting from it.

Q. 4.   Should I ask permission?

   A. Your angels are eager to receive
       this blessing. If you are netting a
       human, the net will not be able to
       land on them if they do not want
       it. Their energy field will deflect it.

It's all good folks. Now, get busy and hurl some
nets!

Here is our chance to show the spirit world that we are awake and ready for the Golden Age of less struggle and more victorious living.

Non-Dominant Handwriting

When you write with the non-dominant hand, you have a direct connection to the right side of the brain. The right side of the brain houses your intuition, your spirituality, and your creativity. The left-brain houses the logical, analytical side. Non-dominant handwriting is an effective way to communicate with your team of Holy Spirit helpers.

Where did I learn the power of Non-Dominant Handwriting?

I invested a year-and-a-half studying directly with Dr. Lucia Capacchioni who has written many books that use journaling and Non-Dominant Handwriting as a form of free therapy. Books like *Power of Your Other Hand* and *Recovery of Your Inner Child* are available on Amazon.

If I could recommend only one technique in the whole wide world to increase psychic awareness, it would be writing with the non-dominant hand. Do it every day for six months and you won't believe your results. Combine this with regular HPT and you will grow by leaps and bounds! It's incredible and it's easy.

The dominant hand is the one you write checks with. It doesn't matter if you're right- or left-handed. The dominant hand is the one you eat with and write checks with. Some people say they are ambidextrous; the one you write checks with is your dominant hand.

- NOTE: Non-dominant handwriting is NOT "automatic writing." A spirit will not possess you and move your hand. This is wisdom that comes from your own self; the right side of your brain. Just write slowly, one word at a time. As you grow accustomed to doing this, Non-Dominant Handwriting will be easier and easier.

And BTW... the right side of the brain has not learned how to lie yet, so you get direct access to a lot of truth by doing this.

Beginner's Exercise

1. Using unlined paper, turn it so it's 'landscape' (wider across the bottom).

2. Write your name with your non-dominant hand.

3. Put the pen back in your dominant hand and ask, "How did that feel writing with my non-dominant hand?"

4. Put the pen in the non-dominant hand and let the answer flow.

Second Exercise

Now you are ready to take Non-Dominant Handwriting a step further and address a sub-personality.

1. With a pen in your dominant hand, write: "Dear Inner Wisdom, how can I move forward on my path more easily?"

2. Put the pen in the non-dominant hand and let the answer flow.

To communicate with your Holy Spirit team, you could do as follows:

1. With your dominant hand, write: "Dear Holy Spirit team, Thank you for being with me. Do you have any blessings for me today?

2. Next, switch the pen to the non-dominant hand and allow the answer to flow one word at-a-time.

You may not get much at first, but continue and you will find advice flows easily!

Please do not ask "fortune telling" questions such as, *What are the winning lottery numbers?* or *Will I meet my true love by Tuesday?*

I promise: Keep it simple and your abilities will grow like crazy!

Sometimes, you might have a very strong inner critic who tells you things like:

- This is so stupid
- You are just making this up
- No-one can read this (no one but you is supposed to read it)

Realize that this is just normal. Proceed anyway.

Coming Soon by Rebecca Marina Messenger

Jesus was Not Born Magic: How He Learned to Do His Miracles, and How You Can Too!

www.ingramcontent.com/pod-product-compliance
Lightning Source LLC
Chambersburg PA
CBHW060943040426
42445CB00011B/983